The Busy Volunteer's

GUIDE
—————— to ——————
FUNDRAISING

*The Truths and Nothing but
the Truths about Raising
Money for Your Cause*

America's Topselling Fundraising Books

Fund Raising Realities
Every Board Member Must Face

A 1-Hour Crash Course on Raising
Major Gifts for Nonprofit Organizations

David Lansdowne

From the first page, you and your board will be hooked on this one-hour-to-read gem.

The warmth, encouragement, the perfectly tuned examples, and easy readability make for an inviting package that draws you in at once.

Without wasting a word, Lansdowne distills the essence of big-gifts fundraising into 43 "realities," and explains each principle and technique in a way board members will understand immediately.

Put this classic in your board's hands, in their orientation packet, in their annual meeting folder, in their workshop handouts. Put it anywhere you need the art of fundraising illuminated in a masterful, uncomplicated, and engaging way.

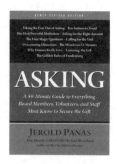

ASKING

A 59-Minute Guide to Everything
Board Members, Volunteers, and Staff
Must Know to Secure the Gift

Jerold Panas

It ranks right up there with public speaking. Nearly all of us fear it. And yet it's critical to the success of our organizations. Asking for money. It makes even the stout-hearted quiver.

But now comes a book, *Asking,* and short of a medical elixir, it's the next best thing for emboldening board members, volunteers, and staff to ask with skill, finesse … and powerful results.

The No. 1 bestselling fundraising book of all time, *Asking* convincingly shows that it doesn't take stellar sales skills to be an effective asker. Nearly everyone can be successful if they follow Panas' step-by-step guidelines.

Emerson & Church, Publishers
www.emersonandchurch.com

The Busy Volunteer's

GUIDE
— to —
FUNDRAISING

*The Truths and Nothing but
the Truths about Raising
Money for Your Cause*

KAY SPRINKEL GRACE

Emerson
& Church
PUBLISHERS

First printed in April 2016

Printed in the United States of America
This text is printed on acid-free paper.

Copies of this book are available from the publisher at discount when purchased in quantity.

Emerson & Church, Publishers
15 Brook Street, Medfield, MA 02052

Tel. 508-359-0019
www.emersonandchurch.com

Library of Congress Cataloging-in-Publication Data

Names: Grace, Kay Sprinkel, author.
Title: The busy volunteer's guide to fundraising : The truths and nothing but the truths about raising money for your cause / Kay Sprinkel Grace.
Description: Medfield, Massachusetts : Emerson & Church, Publishers, [2016]
Identifiers: LCCN 2015051255 | ISBN 9781889102573 (pbk. : alk. paper)
Subjects: LCSH: Fund raising—United States. | Nonprofit organizations—United States—Finance.
Classification: LCC HV41.2 .G7247 2016 | DDC 658.15/224—dc23
LC record available at http://lccn.loc.gov/2015051255

To my late mother, Marian Boyles Sprinkel, who taught me to live my truth. She is still my inspiration.

All truths are easy to understand once they are discovered; the point is to discover them.

—Galileo Galilei

CONTENTS

Contents

Contents

INTRODUCTION

A s a volunteer fundraiser, you've no doubt experienced moments when you weren't sure where to turn for answers. I hope this quick read will become a handy resource for you. Just as much, I hope it'll heighten your enthusiasm for the causes to which you're committed.

Some of the fundraising truths you'll read about are absolute. They are great practice wherever you are and whatever you do. Others may be relative to a community or cause. Regardless, you'll find useful ideas to bolster your confidence.

The discerning reader may see some similarities between this book and a previous work of mine, Fundraising Mistakes That Bedevil All Boards (and Staff Too). I decided not only to turn the focus on volunteer fundraisers, but also to flip the discussion and offer the positive side—in keeping with my great optimism about our sector and its ability to serve our community, our country, and the world.

Thank you for offering your time and talents to the organizations and communities who are counting on you. As one wit put it: "Those who can, do. Those who can do more, volunteer."

Kay Sprinkel Grace
San Francisco, California

Chapter 1

◆

Donors give to your organization because you meet needs, not because you have needs

This is the most important truth in fundraising. Get this one right and the others will be easier to realize.

Think of the most successful philanthropic organizations in the US—our universities, hospitals, and major arts organizations. They don't portray themselves as needy. They present themselves as organizations meeting needs. They showcase their successes. They quantify their impact.

During last decade's economic downturn, I received countless solicitations from organizations bemoaning their budget shortfalls, their tail-spinning annual funds, and the programs sure to be cut without my support. These groups erroneously thought I'd give simply because they had needs. What I wanted to know instead was exactly what societal needs they were addressing.

By contrast, during the same period Stanford University raised more than $6 billion from 160,000 donors.

How was this possible? Certainly, part of the reason is the stature of Stanford. But just as importantly the university presented opportunities for donors to invest in the long-term needs of society such as the environment and energy.

You can do the same by telling the stories of those whose needs you have met. Whatever your cause—whether it's the arts, health, aging, domestic violence, or children's needs—there is no constraint on the hopeful message you can send.

The truth is plain to see: people invest in impact not in needy organizations.

Chapter 2

◆

Fundraising is as much about relationships as it is money

This is the second-greatest truth, and in our hurry to raise money we often forget it.

Successful organizations build and nurture relationships. They rely on volunteers like you to be the bridge to the community, bringing people who share the organization's values into the fold.

You play a critical role, whether it's meeting new people and bringing them to an event, sharing your enthusiasm about an organization over lunch, or listening to a friend talk about something of great importance and realizing that the group for which you volunteer has programs matching your friend's interests and values.

Organizations that hold their ground and even thrive during recessions are those that, with your help, have solid bonds with their donors. Even in bad times, these organizations continue to ask supporters to invest in the successes they've already helped to build. And feeling like partners, donors respond.

For too long we've viewed fundraising as transactional—where all the effort is put into securing the gift and very little into developing a productive relationship. But by forging a partnership with our donors, not only do we communicate the gratitude they're owed, we markedly increase the chances they'll stay with us through both thick and thin times.

Chapter 3

◆

Tax deductibility, which most nonprofits can offer, isn't a powerful incentive

We overemphasize this aspect of giving. How else do you explain the rise of philanthropy in countries where there's little or no tax incentive to give? When asked, donors place tax advantages far down on their list of reasons for giving—after mission, impact, leadership, and opportunities to make a difference.

Some time ago I was in a meeting—we were inviting a donor to invest $1 million in a healthcare organization. Things were going well. The prospective donor was listening carefully and nodding as we shared the vision. We let him know how crucial his gift would be.

And then my colleague chirped in, "And, don't forget—you can write it off."

The donor seemed to deflate immediately. He had listened to our appeal because he wanted to do something important for the community; he wanted to enhance lives and return some of the blessings he'd been given.

Unfortunately, my colleague had reduced the discussion to a financial transaction.

Likewise, I recall a wonderfully generous donor in her 80s who set up an estate gift with her university. Informed of the enormous tax advantage in doing so, she smiled and confessed she'd have to live to be 120 to realize all of the accrued benefits from her philanthropy.

You do need to know a donor's circumstances and how important tax incentives are to him or her. But don't lead off with talk about the IRS, as all charitable nonprofits can offer the same advantage.

Instead, as you listen, try to uncover the donor's motivation for giving and speak to that desire when presenting your project. Only in this way will you ignite the donor's desire to support you for the long term.

Chapter 4

◆

Individuals are the largest source of gifts, not foundations and corporations

Every year, Giving USA reveals that just over 80 percent of charitable gifts in the US come from individuals: about 70 percent from living individuals and another 10 percent from individual's estates.

That leaves approximately 20 percent each year that comes from foundations and corporations combined. Yet the perception remains that these entities are the best sources for large gifts.

Foundations and corporations publicize their giving, which skews our perception. For individuals, only mega gifts receive a similar level of publicity (think Mark Zuckerberg, Michael Bloomberg, and Warren Buffett).

Individuals are a vast and wonderful market. They don't have to consult a committee before making a gift. They can give without restrictions. They'll contribute more than once a year if so moved. They live in the community and are invested in the outcomes.

This explains why identifying and cultivating individual donors is paramount.

There are times in our organizational growth—a pioneering new project comes to mind—when institutional giving from corporations, foundations, and associations is exactly the place to focus. But never at the cost of neglecting the individual gift market where the real action has always been.

Chapter 5

◆

Special events aren't the most effective way to raise money

I t's alarming that even after all the focus on fundraising costs, many still think a special event will be a quick, easy, and lucrative way to close a budget gap.

We keep falling into this trap for two reasons: first, special events mean we don't have to approach our friends and colleagues in person for significant gifts—we can sell a table of ten instead, and, second, from the outside events appear quick and easy.

In reality, special events hover at or near the bottom on the ladder of effective ways to raise money, slightly above advertising (which we'll get to later).

In my first fundraising job, I inherited a calendar of nine modest events and one blockbuster—a symphony concert. In my youthful zeal I seized the opportunity to add another noteworthy event, a splashy wine-tasting party.

Only later did I see the sobering reality. A year-end cost analysis revealed that our net was much lower than we expected and our volunteer burnout considerably higher. Gradually we scaled back and began growing our major individual giving program.

That said, as part of a balanced fundraising program special events can play a key role in raising funds and friends for your organization. I myself feel a signature event is important, something you're known for, that no one wants to miss.

But too many events equate to too much time and money that could be spent more effectively on engaging potential donors, cultivating them in small gatherings, and putting your substantial relationship-building talents into those actions that will result in a major gift *as well as* a lasting relationship.

Chapter 6

◆

To attract donors, you need to tell your organization's story

How wonderful it would be if, because ours is a good cause, people rushed to give. Occasionally that happens with a new organization but the glow quickly fades.

In truth, we have to tell our stories constantly. Fortunately, there have never been more opportunities to tell those stories—and tell them well—than today.

Social media platforms abound and savvy organizations use them. Tweeting is expected; a Facebook page is a must; your website should be vibrant and current; and emails have to be tailored to the recipients' interests and issues (forget email blasts except in rare cases like a broad-scale disaster).

Believing that people will discover how wonderful your group is without marketing yourself is akin to the 1940s Hollywood starlet who thought she'd be discovered by sitting at the soda fountain at Schraft's Drug Store. Maybe it worked for one or two, but as a career strategy it was a failure.

In *Good to Great and the Social Sectors*, Jim Collins proposes a constructive idea. Acknowledging that much of what our sector does can't really be measured, he suggests we gather our statistics—for example, "Last year we served 147 at-risk mothers with our parenting program"—and then tell *one* story of *one* of those mothers to illustrate impact. The person who reads the story will himself or herself multiply that impact by 147.

Tell your truth. Tell your impact. Let your good cause out from under the bushel basket. If you don't turn on the light, who will?

Chapter 7

◆

Donors want to see the measurable impact you're having

Times have changed. A half-century ago people who gave to causes were often called "do-gooders." They contributed and assumed the organization would put the money to good use. No longer. Today's donors expect metrics, transparency, accountability, and return on investment.

Even iconic organizations like the Red Cross and United Way have faced criticism for failing to report their use of contributions. In contrast, Doctors Without Borders earned a huge amount of positive press when, several days after the 2004 South Asian tsunami, it announced it had enough money for relief and was no longer accepting contributions for that purpose.

The decision to give, as we'll discuss later in this book, germinates in the heart and is validated in the head. As a consequence, we should always remember to speak to donors' hearts with our stories, and to their heads with results we can measure.

Trust is the underlying issue. And we hold our donors' trust when we demonstrate that not only are our hearts in the right place but so is our leadership, our measurable impact, and our bottom line.

Chapter 8

◆

Yours doesn't have to be a household name to attract a donor's attention

If you are the YMCA, Goodwill, Big Brothers Big Sisters, or the Sierra Club, you'll have an easier time getting a donor's attention. There's no doubt about that. But if you're *not* one of these brand names, all is not lost.

Today, donors are looking for one crucial factor in their philanthropic investment: impact. They're less concerned about brand and more concerned about an organization's ability to solve problems and enrich lives. If you're a mission-focused, trusted organization, you can get a donor's attention—and keep it—whether or not your brand is widely known.

It's easy to say that all the money went to the Y or the Boys and Girls Club and that's why your campaign didn't do well. But that's disingenuous. If you build relationships, show results, earn the trust of your donors, and keep them engaged, you'll grow your brand recognition, if only locally.

Midway through a big fundraising campaign, a 30-year-old organization decided to change its name. Some worried that brand recognition would fade with the new name. They suggested waiting until the drive was over and the building completed. But the visionary leadership knew that the name they had—though widely recognized—wasn't why people gave. Donors would continue their support because of the organization's policies, programs, and impact.

They were right. The Family Violence Prevention Fund became Futures Without Violence and the campaign didn't miss a beat. People knew what they were investing in: results.

Trust in a brand is important—we see that in the purchases we make. But new brands come on the market all the time. We try them. We like them.

You don't have to have a high-recognition name to be a highly trusted and funded organization. The truth isn't in the name. It's in the result.

Chapter 9

◆

For big gifts you need to ask in person

As crazy as it may seem—and is—there are organizations that send letters seeking large gifts—$25,000, $250,000, or more. I recently learned of a board member dashing off a note for $3 million! But I can guarantee there was a long personal relationship between the asker and the donor before that correspondence.

While social networks, e-mails, and even tailored personal letters have their place, at some point you have to get up close and personal with the prospective donor.

Despite this, we persist in relying on letters or even e-mails for several reasons. One, it means we don't have to put ourselves on the line and face the possibility of rejection or embarrassment. Two, some volunteers insist they can present the case more effectively in a letter (in which case, they should write a letter as a prelude to their visit). Three, and perhaps the only reason for writing a letter or an e-mail, is due to geography. Even then, the correspondence should be the final step in a highly personal solicitation process.

It may sound strange, but once you're practiced at it, asking in person is often enjoyable. You're able to read reactions, adjust your conversation, answer questions, and experience the joy the donor feels when he or she decides to give. How much more exhilarating this is than waiting for the mail carrier to arrive or for the ping of your e-mail.

If fears are getting in your way, ask for coaching. Ask for a partner to go with you. Ask for a bromide if you must. You'll find that the rewards of personally asking trump any fears lurking within you.

Chapter 10

◆

Don't depend on publicity and advertising to raise money

Wouldn't it be great if we only needed to spread the word about our work to have people calling, e-mailing, and dropping by with fistfuls of money?

Crowdsourcing and text appeals during crises are the modern manifestations of this desire. These outreach strategies raise money for special projects but they're not a sustainable source for long-term funding. In fact, if overused, they convey desperation rather than opportunity for long-term investment.

At one point in the early years of philanthropy, advertising was on the list of practices for raising annual dollars. There were magazine and newspaper coupons you could clip and return with your donation. These yielded little and were soon phased out.

Shortly after its founding, Interplast (now ReSurge International), was thrilled to be featured in a national magazine. The article told heartwarming stories of physicians traveling to Latin America to perform life-changing surgeries on children. Accompanying photos offered the visual narrative. At the end of the story there was a "call to action" asking readers to send a donation, with instructions on how to do so. Interplast had hoped such publicity would boost its fundraising. Unfortunately—but predictably—the response was negligible.

The real story here is balance. Yes, we need good publicity. And advertising on the web or in print can sometimes play a role in an overall outreach program. But recognize these measures for what they are: a prelude and reinforcement to the personal overtures needed for successful long-term fundraising.

Chapter 11

◆

People genuinely like to give

This is a truth many struggle with—even professionals in the field. There's a residual undercurrent of belief, a little voice inside, that persuades us people don't *really* like to give.

Granted, some may balk at the amount of your request or need time to consider it, but most people feel joy in giving. The late Hank Rosso, founder of The Fundraising School (now part of the Lilly Family School of Philanthropy at Indiana University) responded to those who asked him about his life's work by saying, "Fundraising is the gentle art of teaching the joy of giving." All these many years later I can vouch for those words.

I recall Denise who gave the largest gift to a capital campaign I was involved with. At the dedication of the building, what struck the board and everyone in the room was the joy and gratitude she expressed for having been offered the opportunity to make it all possible. Moved to tears, she said how much the mission meant to her and what a privilege it was for her to be part of such an amazing vision. Since that gift, Denise has given millions more to support the organization's work.

I've never thought of fundraising as pressure. I think of it as *release*. When fundraising is done right, the donor feels a sense of release. Pent-up dreams and values have found a home at an organization creating something important.

Presenting donors with social-investment opportunities that reflect their desire to make an impact drains the pressure from solicitations. We offer people who share our values an opportunity to act on them—and to trust that together as partners for positive change, we'll transform the situation hand in hand.

Chapter 12

◆

Donors come from
every walk of life

Ambrose Bierce was once asked to describe a philanthropist. His response? "A rich, white, old, bald man." With the democratization of philanthropy, nothing could be further from the truth today.

Philanthropy is now accessible and enjoyed by people of all ages, by people of color, by women, and by those without massive amounts of money.

As citizen-philanthropists—operating from our laptops—we can access thousands of organizations in hundreds of countries dealing with issues from hunger to human rights to equitable education for girls. We can exercise the power of one, no matter who and where we are.

Giving cuts across all demographics and, as a result, the people we approach are a lot like us. They live next door, drive the kids' carpool, compete on the same golf courses, and are waiting in the checkout line next to you. And guess what? Some of them are looking at you and wanting to bring you closer to an organization they care about.

Of course, many donors do reside in the toniest suburban neighborhoods or city penthouses. But they still care about the same things and feel the same frustrations and the same pain as the rest of us.

Philanthropic vision is a leveler. Rich and poor alike suffer from devastating diseases. Disasters know no boundaries. The loss of a child or the aging of a parent is a universal grief. The arts can enrich our lives no matter what our income or assets may be. Threats to the environment are important to all of us.

Few other social magnets draw people together like philanthropy. How lucky we are.

Chapter 13

◆

Even if your worthy cause makes people uncomfortable, you can find support

We all know how easy it is to raise money for children and animals. Heart-wrenching stories, appealing photographs, and celebrity endorsers advance these causes in ways we can only envy.

But if yours is a cause that makes people uncomfortable, if you deal with something many would rather not talk about, or address issues with limited acceptance, you might think you can't raise money.

But in truth you can. Your constituency will be smaller but chances are your donors' shared values and determination will be more intense, and many of these issues are exactly what family foundations and contributors to donor-advised funds like to support.

I once worked with a group that served adult survivors of incest. We were able to raise money because we found there were clusters of people who really cared, from their own experience or from concern about the issue, and they gave.

Likewise, domestic violence was once something spoken of in hushed tones. Now it's a mainstream issue. Organizations working to solve the problem of domestic abuse are faring well.

Your cause doesn't have to be mainstream to thrive. Futures Without Violence, mentioned in chapter 8, found a unique way to engage men in helping to increase awareness of domestic abuse. First, they formed The Founding Fathers, enlisting business, sports, and civic leaders to launch an endowment fund. Then they created a program called "Coaching Boys Into Men," working with high school coaches and athletes around the US, providing training and a playbook to promote respect for girls and women. The program has now been implemented in India and other countries through a partnership with UNESCO.

If yours isn't a cause that evokes oohs and aahs, search for those in whom your issue evokes a passion. Don't worry whether they have wealth. Remember, fundraising isn't about money, it's about relationships based on shared values. If people engage in your cause, they'll link you to others, some of whom will have the resources to advance your work.

Chapter 14

◆

You can raise substantial money even if you don't know any wealthy people

Barack Obama's Internet fundraising success in two presidential races demonstrated that aggregated small gifts can make a huge difference. During his 2008 campaign, Obama attracted more than six million online gifts, averaging $80 and totaling more than $500 million.

Since 2008, we've seen philanthropy shift toward text giving, crowdsourcing, and other techniques that don't rely on large donors. When you total up these gifts, you very well may have a pile of money and a whole list of new donors with whom to build relationships.

Of course, many organizations don't have the staff, resources, or constituencies to pull off an Obama-like fundraising miracle. Moreover, our fickle American population grows weary of constant online and text appeals, so we're seeing some pushback.

The good news is that you can raise big money in traditional fundraising even when you don't know any rich people. But you will need to draw in those who know the rich.

Years ago I guided a $15 million church restoration campaign in a woefully impoverished neighborhood. From the outset, it was clear that none of the people involved was wealthy or knew anyone who was.

To counter this, we began engaging civic, business, and union leaders in a committee to address the importance of restoring the facilities of this nearly city-block campus which served as an oasis for the homeless and working poor.

We expanded our notion of who might contribute and had two versions of our case for support: one for business leaders who would see the importance of restoring this facility that bordered on the commercial district, and another for those who shared the faith and viewed the restoration as a way to advance the ministries.

We dug deeply into records of the church—who was married there in better times, for example. We conducted a unique cultivation event, Margaritas in the Monastery, that captured the attention of people who hadn't visited that part of the city in decades. The brothers served the drinks and guacamole, and prospects came by the hundreds and took the tour. They also gave.

Immigrant members of the congregation— Vietnamese, Filipino, Hispanic—got involved. They fasted, they feasted, and the Hispanic congregants had Friday tamale sales, earmarking all proceeds to the project.

We reached our goal. Our largest gift was $1 million. The smallest, eleven cents, came from someone who wrote his name in perfect Palmer script on a church donation envelope and listed his address as "homeless."

It *is* much harder to raise money if you don't know rich people—and it requires a lot more imagination. But with tenacity, vision, enthusiasm, and systems for reaching out to many who can give small gifts, it positively can be done.

Chapter 15

◆

Giving involves both the head and the heart

In this time of measuring everything, of demands for metrics and quantifiable impact, it's easy to forget the heart plays the pivotal role in people's giving.

A number of years ago, the William and Flora Hewlett Foundation cut short a study that looked at the way individual donors used metrics in their giving decisions. With few exceptions, the study found it was a balance of head and heart, with the heart most often the stronger factor.

What this goes to show is that while metrics, blueprints, and budgets are important and appeal to the donor's rational side, if the heart isn't engaged, if the project isn't aligned with the donor's values, the gift won't happen. Or it will be smaller than hoped for.

In one campaign I was involved with, the board was convinced that a wealthy entrepreneur could be cultivated for the lead gift. To me, it seemed his heart wasn't in the project. I suggested instead that a certain member of the board, who had been making increasingly generous annual gifts, be the lead donor. My idea was dismissed. The board said he had already "given so much they couldn't ask for more."

So, the entrepreneur was wined and dined for nearly a year—all for naught. When the board chair announced we'd have to go back to 'square one' in our quest for the lead gift, the person I originally suggested as the likely donor called the chair and said he was hoping to be asked and would like to make the gift.

I was overjoyed, but not surprised. While there is a business side to every large gift—this one was for eight figures—the genesis comes from the heart and is secured by the head, not the reverse.

We have shied away from the emotional aspect of our causes because of the excesses of some organizations—clubbed seals, vivisected animals, starving children. People turn their heads in shock rather than feeling drawn to support these initiatives. In truth, however, genuine emotion and powerful storytelling is the tool for building credibility and response in our donors.

Chapter 16

◆

Almost everyone is uncomfortable with asking for money

When I ask volunteers if they enjoy asking for money, few raise their hand. Some will qualify their reluctance; others say they'd prefer a hip replacement.

We are conditioned not to ask for money. Asking is a sign that somehow we haven't managed to do well. We're needy, we're beggars.

But remember the first truth of this book: "People give to your organization because you meet needs, not because you have needs." To gain confidence, if not comfort, there are three key facts to keep in mind:

1. You're not asking for yourself, nor are you asking for a needy organization. You're asking on behalf of a successful cause that's meeting needs and is seeking community investment to extend its programs and impact.

2. You aren't begging. The organization is stable, accountable, and successful in its work.

3. You are offering people opportunities to act on their values, to join with you in strengthening an organization that is advancing the things you and they cherish and value in the community.

If you mind your message, you'll find the butterflies leaving your stomach, the calm returning to your body, and the warm invitational language returning to your voice.

Chapter 17

◆

Values, not wealth, determine
a person's willingness to give

We use various criteria to compile our list of would-be donors but the biggest one is usually wealth. "John Taylor just built an enormous house; he obviously has money; let's add him to our list."

Over and over we fail to recognize the obvious. John could be as rich as Gates, but if he doesn't share your values or your vision, he still won't give or he'll give modestly from a sense of duty. We're much better served if we begin with people who share our values.

One performing arts organization I worked with during a slow economy stayed vibrant when others around it stumbled. The executive director engaged her community, identified what types of performances were desired, paid attention to donors at *all* levels, and gave constituents what they valued. Her charitable revenue never went down.

A few years ago, those on the Forbes 400 were asked to name the principal driver of their giving. The

Chronicle of Philanthropy reported that 70 percent identified "personal values." In addition to values, however, there are three other factors we need to consider when identifying someone as a viable prospect for giving:

- a personal connection to the organization,
- concern for the cause, and
- financial capacity to give.

Although common sense tells us the first two outweigh the third, we persist in starting with the third.

Invariably when I'm working with an organization on a campaign, someone will hand me a list of people to interview for a feasibility study or to invite to a cultivation event. When I ask how these individuals are allied with the organization, more often than not the answer is, "They aren't—but they have money."

When generating new lists, resist the temptation to have fellow volunteers scribble down all the high-net-worth individuals in town. Instead, start by asking, "Who in the community shares our values and is interested in our work?"

Chapter 18

◆

There are no "right words" when asking

How tedious it would be if we all carried the same script when calling on prospective donors! And what if all of us used the same foundation proposal, and all fundraising letters, emails and tweets were nearly identical? What a dreary landscape that would produce!

While there are certain phrases that work better than others—for example, inclusive language such as "join with us," "be part of," or "I know from our conversations that you and I share a belief in . . . ,"—even these phrases can be set aside if you have a better way of saying the same thing and achieving the right outcome.

The only "right words" are those that reflect you and your organization, and those you know are right for the donor because you've been an attentive listener and discerned what he or she cares about.

Calling on a prospective donor so much depends on the relationship between the two (or three) of you.

Remember, you're having a conversation. You have to be yourself and it has to feel natural.

To be sure, you'll want to remember what you learned in your training or coaching sessions and it's a good idea to avoid phrases such as "Anything you can give will be great" or "I'm sorry to be bothering you."

Keep in mind, too, that words won't flow perfectly. My favorite illustration of this truth: One volunteer, intimidated by a would-be donor who was much older and in a higher position in the same company, finally asked the man for the gift—$25,000. He seemed stunned and said no one had ever asked him for a gift of that size. She blurted out the first thing that came to her mind: "Well, I've never ASKED anyone for a gift that size." They both laughed . . . and he wrote the check.

Chapter 19

◆

You have to give
before you can ask

We've all heard about time equaling money. No
doubt it does for professionals who charge by
the hour—attorneys, for instance. But with respect to
philanthropic work we need to dispense with this notion
once and for all.

Time doesn't substitute for money in our sector. If we
all gave time alone, how would our organizations serve
capably in the community, much less pay the utility bill?

Similarly, I've heard about those who get their company to donate $10,000 while giving nothing themselves,
thinking their gift has been covered by the $10,000.
The old canard "Give or get" has no place in my book
of truths—it is "give AND get."

This truth bears repeating: you cannot seek gifts if
you haven't given. There are two primary reasons:

1. You can't ask others to "join with you" with
   authenticity when in fact you're not among those
   who have given.

2. Outside funders—non-board individuals, foundations, corporations—will all want to know there's been 100 percent giving from your board AND from your development or campaign committee. Otherwise, why should they pitch in?

Here's something equally important: A funny thing happens when you write your own check. Not only does it feel good, it also deepens your commitment to the cause. Suddenly you become a vocal advocate and want everyone else to feel as good. Your enthusiasm becomes contagious. Hank Rosso used to say, "You have to get religion if you are going to preach religion."

And remember that donors are sharp. They'll often question you about your own support. If you, who are closest to the organization, haven't made a financial commitment, your appeal to them is an empty one. "Come back when you've decided what you're going to give," they very well might say.

Understand this, too: As a volunteer you should expect to be asked for an annual gift and for an additional gift during special campaigns. This ask should be personal, in a meeting with the board chair and CEO. Only then, in the context of your service being acknowledged and your ongoing role in the organization discussed, will the request for your gift mimic the request you'll eventually make of others.

You too deserve to experience the joy of giving.

Chapter 20

♦

Always ask
for a specific amount

I t's true. In almost all cases, you'll ask for a specific amount.

In my work as a volunteer leader for various organizations, this is one of the toughest instructions for people to follow. And in my work as a campaign consultant, it's the directive volunteers question more than any.

Askers worry that naming a specific amount reveals to would-be donors that a log of personal information has been gathered about them—net worth, real estate holdings, giving history, gifts to other organizations. It is true. Such data is called prospect research. Askers fear, too, that citing a number will cause surprise, resentment, or anger.

Step aside for a moment and look at it from the donor's perspective. If you've approached things right, the person you're calling upon is acquainted with your cause, knows the purpose of your visit, has agreed to meet with you, and, chances are, is a savvy donor used to these solicitation calls. The biggest unknown to him or her is simply how much you're seeking.

I have been on calls when someone on our team would say, "And so, Charlie, we hope you'll consider being part of this effort to build a community theater and that you'll make a significant gift."

Significant gift. What does that mean? $5,000? $50,000? $500,000? You must name a specific amount— or, if not an exact amount, at least a range.

Most capital campaigns, and many annual campaigns, use either a gift range chart or a list of naming opportunities ("For a gift of $125,000, this room will bear the name of your loved one").

Some askers, uncomfortable with citing a figure, will hand the chart to the prospect. "We were hoping you'd consider making a leadership gift in the range of $10,000 to $25,000. Is that something you will consider?" Not as good as asking for $25,000 outright, but better than being completely vague.

Be as specific as you can with your request. Rather than being resentful, the would-be donor will respect your preparation and that your organization has a good back-office operation—one that'll also keep track, and make efficient use, of his or her gift once it's made.

Chapter 21

◆

You can ask donors to give more than once a year

When individuals become donors, they have a keen interest in protecting their investments. So when opportunities arise to strengthen the organization further, your donors are the first people to whom you should turn—even if they've already made their annual gifts.

Understand, I'm not talking about unceasing solicitations—donors dislike that. Some years back, a Cygnus Research study of North American donors reported that the main reason people stopped giving was that they were "solicited too much."

But if you have a major donor who loves your work, and for whom your cause is a top philanthropic priority, don't hesitate to ask if the new opportunity is one he or she would like to fund.

In my first fundraising job, I was working with a generous donor who had already made the largest annual gift we'd received that year ($25,000). One day, she stopped by my office and asked how things were going—particularly with the initiative she was most fond of. Excitedly, I told her the teachers in the program had come to me with an amazing discovery—early reading books that were specifically designed for children with learning disabilities. She was intrigued and asked for more information. When I said I was thinking of approaching one of our corporate donors for the funds to purchase the books ($7,500), she took out her checkbook on the spot!

It was a key lesson I've never forgotten. Now I advise organizations to identify who among their active donors might be interested in the opportunity at hand. I encourage them to call the individual, describe the project, and say, "I wanted to give you the chance to fund this because I know it's something you care about. I realize you just made your annual gift but I felt that you'd share our excitement over this idea—so I decided to call you first."

It doesn't always result in a gift, but most of the time the donor chooses to contribute.

One way many organizations are encouraging people to give many times during the year is monthly or sustained giving. Public television and radio stations are masters at this: the $60 or larger gift is spread out over twelve months and then automatically renewed.

Sustained giving is on the rise and is worth exploring. Planned Parenthood, Habitat for Humanity, and countless others have realized that this approach encourages donors to give more and boosts the organization's cash flow throughout the year.

Chapter 22

◆

Staff aren't always the right or the best askers

As our sector has become more professional—especially in higher education, health care, and large arts organizations—we've increasingly given the job of asking to our fundraising staffs.

As a result, I've heard volunteers express relief when an organization's first development director is hired, saying now they won't have to go out and ask for money.

But this isn't the case. In truth, our donors would rather speak with a volunteer. It's even better when that volunteer is accompanied by a member of the staff.

Your fundraising officers, if you have them, may be thoroughly trained in asking and have a reservoir of facts and information about the organization. But these advantages pale in comparison to having you, a volunteer, do the asking.

First, as a volunteer you bring a particular passion and perspective to the conversation. It's not your paid job. You don't have to show up, yet you do. Your involvement lends great credibility to the organization.

Second, as noted in chapter 18, asking for money isn't about personal eloquence or voicing the right words. It's about relationships, respect, and influence. It is the rare staff person who travels in the same social circles as his prospective donors.

Finally, in the mind of the prospective donor, a fundraising officer is paid to ask. In fact, his or her livelihood is tied up with getting a "yes." You on the other hand are in the unassailable position of having nothing to gain from your visit except the satisfaction of furthering a cause you believe in and the joy of having another person join you in the organization's work.

You're every bit as effective in asking as the fundraising officer. And, as a team, the two of you are all but unstoppable.

Chapter 23

◆

Ethical consultants and fundraising hires don't bring with them a list of people to solicit

A colleague, who had worked at a major hospital during its fund drive, was hired by another organization at the close of its capital campaign.

When she arrived on the job, the board and CEO said, "Did you bring the list?" My friend was incredulous. She thought they were kidding. The board chair and CEO wanted her to begin "working" the list of people who had contributed to the hospital's campaign. After a few months, my colleague resigned.

Carrying a list of prospects from one organization to another is a breach of fundraising ethics. Why? Because individuals on the list have relationships with specific organizations. Traveling lists treat donors like a commodity instead of as investors motivated by mission and shared values.

With so much information available on various databases, donor names aren't hard to come by. Many contributor lists are posted online in a PDF or annual report. That isn't the issue. The unethical part is expecting a fundraising officer or consultant to provide a researched list to the new organization.

But even apart from this, if your organization has little in common besides its location, then donors on the list may not share your values and wouldn't be good prospects anyway.

There *are* ethical practices in this regard. If you have prospects in your database who are being actively cultivated and have a relationship with you already, it is perfectly ethical for your consultant or new fundraising hire to offer insights, comments, and strategies based on his or her knowledge of the person. They may even suggest a name to you based on their connections in the community or provide insights into someone on the list based on personal experience.

But don't expect consultants or new staff to bring a list with them from another organization: if you do, your own ethics will be called into question.

Chapter 24

◆

It takes money to raise money in a campaign

The bad news: You can't undertake a sizable fundraising campaign without increasing spending on donor and fund development.

The good news: For a properly run campaign, fundraising costs will be less than 10 percent of the total dollars you raise.

What usually causes angst is that the costs will be front loaded. You need attractive materials, new web design elements, additional help in donor tracking, and perhaps even a new staff person.

There's also the matter of training. I've known volunteers to limp along in their solicitations because the organization wouldn't hire a trainer to help them learn effective ways to state the case, rescue a foundering solicitation, and handle objections.

To be sure, a fundraising drive isn't the place for extravagance. But neither is it a time for penny-pinching. If you fail to fund the infrastructure, your effort will take longer—a lot longer, I've found—and may never succeed.

I know from experience that this is hard money for board members to allocate. They argue it isn't program related. At the same time, unless your campaign gains traction, many of your programs may be in jeopardy as a result.

Some will advise using the first money raised to fund the campaign. What that cautious "wait and see attitude" usually bespeaks is a lack of confidence, or worse, a lack of commitment.

A major endeavor deserves appropriate investment. If that isn't forthcoming, you'd be smarter to delay your campaign than have it sputter along and eventually fail.

Chapter 25

◆

You don't need a powerful board of directors to be successful with fundraising

There are organizations across America—particularly universities, hospitals, and large cultural organizations—whose boards are the envy of all. Their members are leaders in commerce, industry, and law who possess wealth and connections in abundance. Annually they provide leadership gifts of six and seven figures, and during capital drives their gifts often constitute as much as 80 percent of the total goal.

If this doesn't describe your core group, join the crowd. For every nonprofit so blessed, there are thousands upon thousands more like yours.

These organizations are governed by people who care deeply about the mission, bring what wealth and connections they have, and are willing to work to fulfill the vision.

You can certainly have a successful campaign with such a core group. The challenge is to form a steering committee made up of several board members and volunteers as well as high-profile leaders in the community. This group will largely be responsible for the campaign's success and regularly report back on the progress being made.

I've found that movers and shakers may not want to join a board, or be involved on an ongoing basis, but they will participate in a campaign limited to a specific time period if they have passion for the project.

For years, religious organizations have used this approach with great success and social service agencies often form campaign leadership committees that involve board and non-board volunteers.

Power is a relative concept. Enlist the right people, even if they're not in your core group, and suddenly your organization will have the potential to raise substantial sums of money.

◆

Chapter 26

Everyone has to be involved in resource development: volunteers, board, and staff

"Not me. I'm dreadful at it."
"You can't be serious. I couldn't sell cheese to a mouse."

"All things being equal, I'd prefer the guillotine."

I'm sympathetic, but no volunteer is off the hook when it comes to resource development.

I didn't say *fundraising.* I said *resource development.* There is a difference.

In truth, everyone needs to be involved in raising money but not everyone has to ASK. That's right. Leaving the asking to a fundraising committee is frequently done, but no sensible organization leaves volunteers out of the full development process.

Resource development is the process of identifying and cultivating potential donors, then maintaining relationships with these individuals once they've made a gift. *Fundraising* focuses on the actual ask.

One volunteer I worked with, Carol, insisted she'd "do anything but ask for money." I surprised her when I said that was all right. Then I asked Carol how she saw herself helping. "Well, I know lots of people," she said, "and I have good lists." That was indeed the case. We used Carol's lists extensively when we held our cultivation events.

At the end of the campaign, we were able to tell her that nearly one-third of what we had raised had come from those who were on her lists. Many of them said they had given because of Carol.

Although you may not have the courage or confidence to ask for a gift yourself, you do have to accept responsibility for aiding and abetting in the most productive way you can.

Chapter 27

◆

Focus on all donors,
not just big donors

Too often I hear organizations say they don't have the resources or time to concern themselves with small donors, other than send a receipt for their gift. These same organizations turn around and tell me their churn rate is very high—that donors aren't renewing.

Connect the dots.

Anyone who contributes is interested in your cause and has the potential to become more involved by giving again or participating in another way.

When you focus only on those who write large checks, you jeopardize your fiscal health in years to come. Giving is cyclical. Those who contribute smaller amounts in their thirties may well become major donors as they grow older. And these same modest givers will in all probability be your planned gift donors in their later years.

When you ignore donors whose gifts don't reach some internal benchmark you've set—say, $200—you lose sight of the following:

1. Anyone, regardless of the size of their gift, can become a champion for you. Astute organizations understand this. No matter how the economy sags or giving becomes sporadic, they keep these donors engaged.
2. Giving levels aren't absolute. There are donors for whom a gift of $100 represents a greater share of income than another's $1,000 gift. When we fail to reach out to smaller donors, we minimize their gifts and disrespect their commitment to our organization.
3. Donors test us. They dip their toe in the water and may make a smaller initial gift to gauge how they'll be treated by you.

Extend your gratitude as deeply into your donor base as you can. Encourage board members and other volunteers to do quarterly thank-a-thons. Send a thank-you, not merely an acknowledgment, to every donor.

Not only will you communicate a great deal about your organization's values but you'll create legions of new champions as well.

Chapter 28

♦

Estate gifts come from donors at all levels

This truth always surprises people. They think estate gifts only come from major donors. But how often have we read about the $25 donor who leaves $1 million to the local animal shelter, or the decades-lapsed donor whose estate provides hundreds of thousands of dollars to an organization where she was once active.

Not so many years ago, a homeless man in Phoenix left an estate of $4 million—including charitable gifts of $400,000 to National Public Radio and other organizations.

In his will, he asked that these words be said when his gift was acknowledged on the air: "Support for NPR comes from the estate of Richard Leroy Walters, whose life was enriched by NPR and whose bequest seeks to encourage others to discover public radio."

One nonprofit I know had a loyal volunteer, a retired schoolteacher whose annual gift never exceeded $100, put her modest house in a trust to benefit the organization.

When she died years later, the property values in her community had soared. Her house, for which she had paid $10,000 sixty years earlier, commanded more than $1 million.

Why did she do it? Because whenever she thought of the future of the children's services agency where she had volunteered for forty years, she wanted to be part of it. Her legacy, invested prudently and supporting programs in perpetuity, ensures that she is.

Chapter 29

◆

You can raise money even if you don't have a stable of annual donors

S ounds far-fetched but it's true. Certainly, a big-dollar campaign is easier if you have an established group of yearly donors. But I know plenty of organizations that succeeded without such a base.

One food bank I worked with had a limited number of annual donors, but because of its visibility, its reputation for sound management, and a growing understanding that better food distribution was needed, the organization convinced would-be donors that a new facility was needed. People who had never given before invested at high levels.

Another organization, which focuses on key environmental issues, had a slim cadre of donors when we started the campaign. We rolled annual giving into a comprehensive drive, resulting in some astounding gifts and a big increase in yearly supporters.

An even more extreme example is an independent high school in Southern California that raised $34 million for the initial phase of its campaign *two years before the school enrolled its first student.* The leadership was strong, the promise was great, the values were clear, and the community rallied to help create this new opportunity for its young people.

Don't let the lack of an annual giving program discourage you from launching a campaign for a building, program, or endowment. With a bold vision, strong leadership, a compelling case, and a solid plan, you can still raise the money you need.

Chapter 30

◆

Asking for a gift that's too big is as bad as asking for one too small

In a way it's flattering to be asked for a large gift, even when we can't afford it. We all like to appear prosperous, I imagine. But that doesn't mean you should ask for an unsupportable amount. Vastly overreaching a person's giving capacity makes you look foolish and creates doubts about your organization's credibility.

If someone has never given more than $1,000 and his or her largest capital gift to *any* cause was $25,000, you will err—and embarrass the donor perhaps—by asking for $100,000, unless recent circumstances, such as an inheritance, have changed his or her capacity to give.

But don't ask for too little, either. If someone has a philanthropic pattern of giving at a certain level, don't make assumptions and lowball your request ("That new sunroom cost plenty," or "I know you just helped your daughter with a down payment on her house"). You'll get the reduced amount. Quickly.

An executive director told me she was about to visit a potential donor with whom the organization had a good relationship but who the director felt would give no more than $100,000. Based on my own conversations with the individual involved, I suggested asking for $100,000 per year over three years for a $300,000 gift. And that was what the donor gave.

As a volunteer leader, I was stunned one time to be asked for a gift of $20,000. At the time, I had children in college and my income was comparatively modest. I had planned to give $10,000 in the form of $2,000 a year for five years. I weighed my feelings about the organization and my own leadership role in the campaign and ended up giving $15,000 over five years.

Stretch is good. Pie in the sky is not.

Chapter 31

◆

We have no right to prejudge a donor's willingness or ability to give

Year after year I've sat in meetings during which potential donors were being identified and reviewed, and over and over I've heard volunteers say:

- "Oh, they can't give. They don't have any money."
- "Them? They're paying off a pledge to their university, and they won't be able to give."
- "Their daughter's wedding is next month. They've got to be tapped out."

Why do we insist on crossing names off lists before we've ever introduced the idea of giving to the people we're deleting?

Think of the consequences. You risk offending someone who may *want* to be asked. And you miss the opportunity of connecting a person with your organization, even if this isn't the right time for him or her to give.

Years ago, when I was the volunteer chair for an educational drive, my steering committee and I hit the fourth year of a five-year campaign. We were drained.

We debated whether to continue asking in a very personal way or to surrender some potential donors to direct mail and telephone. We even discussed whether it was necessary to call on everyone if we reached our goal before contacting all of our prospects.

Then Diane, one of our steering committee members, related this story. In her hometown there was a gala dedication of a new cultural center. With her husband away, Diane invited a friend to accompany her. The friend hesitated and said she wasn't interested. Sensing something was wrong, Diane gently probed. It turned out the woman was resentful because no one had ever asked her for a gift to the new center, and she felt their campaign leadership had assumed she couldn't give.

This sobering story helped us stay the course, exceed our goal, and reach out to more than 90 percent of the people we had been assigned.

Only a donor should tell you whether he or she can give.

Chapter 32

◆

Not all campaigns require a feasibility study

You may not need a feasibility study to conduct a successful campaign. These studies, during which a consultant speaks at length with board and community representatives about an organization's image, its proposed campaign, and the likelihood of the interviewee contributing, used to be standard preparation for any large campaign. Today, more and more organizations are going forward without one.

The reasons vary. Some groups understand full well that, no matter what the study shows, they must proceed anyway. The school has to be expanded. The roof needs to be replaced. The birthing unit must be built.

Other agencies, having delayed their campaigns because of the recommendations of previous studies, feel they now have enough information to go forward without yet another.

Still other organizations consider the study's $15,000 to $50,000 cost prohibitive and are convinced they'll succeed without one.

Lastly, a growing number of agencies are identifying leadership gifts in the early stages of their campaigns and securing handshake commitments from the very beginning.

I'm not against feasibility studies when appropriate. I have conducted scores of them. But if you have engaged your donors, are confident of the way you're perceived in the community, and know where your lead gifts are coming from, your success won't hinge on one. Use the funds instead to add a campaign manager. Then get started with your fundraising.

Chapter 33

◆

All volunteers need fundraising training specific to their organization

Sometimes you may want to slide out of a training session by letting staff know you've already been schooled in asking by other organizations. Although your prior training may have been superb and many of the principles could be the same, you still need training in how to ask for *this* particular organization.

First, you need to know the case for support. Why should someone support this cause? Training will let you test approaches with fellow volunteers in a safety zone so you'll have more confidence when you try them for real.

Second, you don't want to be caught with your facts down. You need to know how many clients your organization serves, when it was founded, what the budget is, and the overall objectives. You also need to be able to articulate the vision. You can't learn these things in someone else's training session.

Third, you need to know the answers to tough questions. You may have to respond to objections, and it's best to have those answers handy.

If those reasons aren't enough, you'll get to know your fellow solicitors better as a result of this training. It's quite possible you'll identify the right person to team up with to make your calls more effective.

As I've said elsewhere in these pages, the most important element in any solicitation is to be yourself, to converse naturally. But by no stretch does that mean flying by the seat of your pants.

Chapter 34

◆

All gifts deserve
heartfelt gratitude

G ratitude should never be calibrated to the size of
a gift.

To be sure, the more a donor gives, the more an
organization should invest in him or her with perks.
But we're out of balance with the nature of philanthropy
when we neglect lower-level donors by offering only a
gift receipt or automated acknowledgment. Or, worse,
when we delay thanking them.

I once found a three-week-old check for $3,000 on
the desk of a staff member. When I asked about the
check, the staffer said she didn't know in which account
to deposit the gift since it exceeded the amount for the
organization's direct mail tracking. I insisted she call the
donor, as I stood there, and explain what had happened.

We miss so many opportunities. One year, I filled
in for the fundraising staff at a client organization as
year-end gifts were pouring in. To my dismay, when
I asked to see the thank-you letters, I was shown

computer-generated acknowledgments. Suddenly I understood clearly why this group had an unusually low rate of retaining donors.

Whether you organize thank-a-thons in which volunteers call donors at all levels, write personal notes, or even send short, *personalized* computer-generated letters, you're showing your donors you genuinely care for their gifts. That's the only way to build relationships and earn your donors loyalty and lasting support.

An Estonian proverb resonates with me: "Who does not thank for little, will not thank for much."

Chapter 35

◆

Those who support organizations with similar missions are likely to support yours

One of the best ways to identify support for your theater is to find lists of donors who support other theaters. It's the same for the environment, animal welfare, education, and the visual arts. Philanthropy is driven by issues and values, not by organizations and their needs.

Recently I had breakfast with a friend who complained, "I gave to the whales and now I'm hearing from the dolphins, gorillas, and pandas!" When I asked if he was supporting these other organizations, he said "Of course I am. I love animals."

If a person is already giving to an organization that brings music to schools, he or she is in fact the most likely person to give to another organization with the same goal.

We're not stealing donors when we approach supporters of like-minded causes. Our mission is bigger than our organization and it takes more than one group to address the issues in our society.

If you peruse the lists of donors from similar organizations in your community, you'll see significant overlap. Once, as we were ramping up to raise money for an arts organization, we collected dozens of program books and annual reports. We singled out the names of donors at certain levels and compared those names against our existing lists. No surprise—we found many shared donors.

Don't worry about "poaching"—you don't have that kind of power. The person you approach decides for herself where to direct her philanthropy. All you're doing is presenting another opportunity.

Chapter 36

◆

Fundraising has multiple objectives

S uccess in fundraising isn't measured in dollars alone, although raising money is the prime purpose, of course.

Enhancing visibility is a second aim. A successful campaign allows you to disseminate your message widely and reach potential supporters who currently aren't on your radar screen.

Engaging more donors of all types and sizes is the third goal. In any major drive, you'll find yourself supported by friends of friends, a volunteer's next-door neighbor, or the granddaughter of an early benefactor. All of these people could prove invaluable in the future as volunteers, donors, or advocates.

Finally, taking the organization to the next level is the ultimate objective of any fundraising push. It is, after all, the reason you're raising money in the first place. From this point forward, your hospital will serve the community more capably, your school's endowment will ensure a higher level of diversity through scholarship support, your homeless shelter will accommodate families as well as single women, or your orchestra's newly endowed chairs will attract the top musicians.

Strangely enough, when you understand the non-monetary and long-term benefits of a well-executed campaign, raising the money becomes a wee bit easier.

Chapter 37

◆

You may need a consultant even if you have fundraising staff

S taff can't do everything all the time. Sometimes you have to call in an expert with a fresh perspective or talents you lack.

Understandably, organizations may resist this additional cost. But there are times when a consultant's perspective isn't only useful but required:

1. Campaign feasibility study. If you choose to do one, it should be conducted by an outsider. These one-on-one interviews with board members, business leaders, and others in the community are more candid and confidential if undertaken by someone not affiliated with the organization.

2. Strategic planning. Whether for the fundraising department or for the entire organization, launching this important process is best left to an outside facilitator—someone free to challenge, stretch, and ignite the thinking of volunteers and staff.

3. Fundraising audit. A periodic, unbiased review of your fundraising practices is an important checkup for improving the ways in which you raise money. Due to vested interests in their jobs and the prominent roles they've played in developing strategies and materials, staff can't be expected to conduct an objective audit.

4. Web design or other technology needs. Today, practically every organization needs a dynamic website, but may not have a staff person to design and oversee it. In this case, hiring someone from the outside is prudent.

Often consultants will relieve internal pressure and also provide an external, objective perspective on the next best steps for your organization.

Chapter 38

◆

Even in today's fast-paced world, most donors still want to be cultivated

With cash in hand, a whole new generation of potential donors has arrived, searching for dreams in which to invest. They're eager if not impatient to see results from their gifts.

At first glance, it may appear today's donors want us to cut to the chase and simply ask them for their gifts. That's not really the case, at least in my experience. Most still need to be involved in your work before they'll contribute to any substantial degree.

Those most likely to shun cultivation and hurriedly make their gift may be young people with new wealth. They've done their research and they know what they want to do.

Others may be old-school fundraising volunteers, steeped in the tradition of philanthropy. They routinely support each other's causes and don't need to be wined and dined.

Except for these specific types, it's best to assume all others want to be cultivated. They want to get to know you, understand your organization, discover shared values, and learn how they can be involved in your work.

If you approach these would-be donors too soon, they may turn you down or give much less than they're capable of giving.

Chapter 39

◆

If your organization is struggling in its campaign, reexamine your case and your methods

I f you have a solid campaign plan in place but your fundraising is stuck, it's time to stop and take stock.

Step back from the sting of rejection and take a "cold water" look at the prospects you've called on. If they were supposed to be your most likely donors and they haven't given, examine why your appeals aren't appealing.

It may be the way you asked or who did the asking. Or it may be something having nothing to do with you—an illness, unforeseen expenses, a drop in corporate revenue or personal income.

Have the courage to revisit those who turned you down and uncover why. Sometimes what we hear as "No" is really "No, not now," or "No, not for that amount."

I remember some years ago when a donor who had pledged more than $2 million backed away from his commitment due to a plunge in net worth. It was a huge blow to the campaign.

Although the organization was discouraged, we didn't give up. Several board members reviewed options with the individual and he eventually agreed to pay quarterly installments over several years. This plan worked for the donor, who felt his assets would recover during the payment period. And it worked for the organization: it kept the campaign alive and provided vital cash flow for their work.

Once you know why your first attempts failed, it can be helpful for everyone involved in the campaign to ask three questions:

1. "Will it make a difference to the community if we abandon this program or project?" If it won't make a difference, then it's doubtful your campaign had merit in the first place. You're probably right to give it up.

2. "Have we made the case in a compelling way—is it urgent, relevant, and exciting to the community?" If not, it's time to sharpen your message, perhaps using feedback from those who initially rejected you.

3. "Do we have other potential donors we can approach, with the goal of engaging them to bring others into the campaign?" If so, then you might postpone your campaign in favor of identifying and cultivating other potential supporters.

Unless there's hard evidence that your campaign is ill conceived, giving up on it should be your last resort.

Chapter 40

◆

Don't expect a windfall gift, but be ready in case it comes

Miracles do happen in philanthropy. Windfall gifts, like casino winnings, become legendary. My life has been peppered with such stories:

- The woman who walked into the housing program with a $25,000 check in hand.
- The church that found $30,000 in the collection plate with a note saying, "I thought it was time I did something for the restoration campaign."
- The individual who came on a field trip to a restored historic site and gave a check for $10,000 "because I haven't helped yet."
- The cathedral that received notice of a $1 million estate gift from the surviving partner of a parishioner who had died many years before.
- And the bequest no one knew anything about until the lawyer called asking where the $700,000 should be sent.

In truth, many organizations will receive some surprise gifts. But of course you can't expect godsends or inflate revenue projections based on previous windfalls.

You still have to plan for every gift, which means compiling lists of potential donors, determining how much they can give, educating them about your organization, and drawing them closer to your work.

Not as thrilling as a gift dropping from the sky, but a lot more dependable.

Chapter 41

◆

The more you do it, the more rewarding fundraising is

You may not believe this, but the more fundraising you do, the more you'll like it. And that makes things easier. You learn how to keep the conversation flowing, how to handle objections, how to phrase your request for a gift. And you see the sheer joy the donor experiences the moment your dream connects with hers.

Of course we all struggle on a personal level with fundraising. It's a continual challenge dealing with the possibility of failure, and embarrassment, and rejection. After a lot of practice, the impact of these factors will lessen, but they never vanish completely.

On a second, broader level, fundraising is daunting because of what's at stake: the orchestra's next season, the solution to a key environmental issue, the care for your community's frail elderly, delivering a little bit of joy to children with cancer, or scholarships for bright students eager for an education.

When you think in this way, fundraising is no longer about you. Or even about your organization. It's about the people who will benefit. Organizations aren't the end users of the gifts we raise. A gift *to* you is really a gift *through* you into the community.

You'll meet some who claim to love asking and show little hesitation about it. Perhaps this even describes you. But even here a word of caution is needed: Always approach fundraising with the respect it deserves. Know everything you can about your prospect and about the organization you represent. Be ready to answer hard questions. Show your respect by listening intently and responding appropriately. Every solicitation has to be as right as you can make it.

Once you get the hang of asking, it does get easier. But even seasoned pros look upon each solicitation with a modicum of fear and a lot of respect. As volunteers, we should do the same.

Chapter 42

◆

There's plenty of philanthropy
to go around

Although there's certainly competition for philanthropic dollars, seldom is it a reason why organizations fail to raise the money they need. In my experience over more than three decades, the wells have never been fuller.

A $100 million naming gift for the UCSF Children's Hospital in San Francisco was recently matched with another $100 million gift from the same donor for a second children's hospital across the bay in Oakland.

Consult The Wall Street Journal, the New York Times, or the Washington Post and you'll see frequent reports about such gifts.

This rise in mega gifts has paralleled the rise in the number of nonprofits—now more than 1.5 million, according to IRS data. And as long as organizations can demonstrate they're meeting community needs and are fiscally sound, donors will continue to invest.

If you're feeling as though the well has run dry for your group, maybe you haven't lowered the dipping bucket to the next level. It's possible your fundraising strategies need to be reviewed. How deliberate and thoughtful is your outreach to donors? How genuine is your stewardship? Are you marketing your impact in the community? Are you staffed adequately to compete in a crowded marketplace? Are there opportunities for collaboration with similar organizations?

In all likelihood, doubts about your securing a healthy share of philanthropy are doubts about your organization's ability to do what's necessary to raise money in today's competitive climate.

By no means have the wells run dry.

Chapter 43

◆

We're public benefit corporations, not charities

There is nothing wrong with the idea of charitable giving. In fact, it's at the heart of the IRS exclusions included in our 501(c)(3) designation.

But the word *charity* no longer captures the innovative aspects of our sector. In reality we are public benefit corporations, even though most of our own professional journals persist in referring to us as charities, as do such mainstream publications like The New York Times.

Today's philanthropists think of themselves as donor-investors. They're looking for a return. They're more demanding, metrics are increasingly important, and innovation is crucial.

Charity has always connoted a handout, not a hand up. We need to let go of that label. It makes us feel less effective than other sectors of our economy. But in truth, we *are* effective. In fact, we've changed the world and we will continue to do so.

Only let us do so with a new name.

A Final Word

There are only two mistakes one can make along the road to truth; not going all the way, and not starting.
—Buddha

There is another saying: that you shall know the truth, and the truth shall make you free. It is my hope these truths will give you the freedom to know what works, what is possible, and what matters in fundraising.

This book reflects my experience. The chapters are testament to the truths I have tested and to those I've observed in countless organizations.

I recall the board member who persuaded her CEO that, yes, they could ask for $1 million from a certain couple, even though others on the board had decided "they probably don't have that kind of money." It literally took less than a minute for the couple to say "Yes."

I remember the young man who attended a workshop and realized he had a "widow's mite" donor waiting to be reached out to with gratitude. He did, and the organization was blessed with a large estate gift.

I observed organizations during the recession that, having learned the truth about caring for all donors, no matter the size of their gifts, stayed strong. They also knew the truth that fundraising isn't about money, but about relationships. They nurtured the relationships, and the money kept coming.

And I have seen boards and volunteers that flourished in the capable hands of a fundraising director who knew how to tap into their motivations and engage them in resource development as ambassadors, advocates, and askers.

I hope that in this book you have discovered some truths and tips that will help you and your organization be inordinately successful.

That is my wish and my purpose in writing it.

The Truths and Nothing But the Truths

A Two-Minute Review

- Donors give to your organization because you *meet* needs, not because you have needs.
- Fundraising is as much about relationships as it is money.
- Tax deductibility, which most nonprofits can offer, isn't a powerful incentive.
- Individuals are the biggest source of gifts, not foundations and corporations.
- Special events aren't the most effective way to raise money.
- To attract donors, you need to tell your organization's story.
- Donors want to see the measurable impact you're having.
- Yours doesn't have to be a household name to attract a donor's attention.

- For big gifts, you need to ask in person.
- Don't depend on publicity and advertising to raise money.
- People genuinely like to give.
- Donors come from every walk of life.
- Even if your worthy cause makes people uncomfortable, you can find support.
- You can raise substantial money even if you don't know any wealthy people.
- Giving involves both the head and the heart.
- Almost everyone is uncomfortable with asking for money.
- Values, not wealth, determine a person's willingness to give.
- There are no "right words" when asking.
- You have to give before you can ask.
- Always ask for a specific amount.
- You can ask donors to give more than once a year.
- Staff aren't always the right or the best askers.
- Ethical consultants and fundraising hires don't bring with them a list of people to solicit.
- It takes money to raise money in a campaign.
- You don't need a powerful board of directors to be successful with fundraising.
- Everyone has to be involved in resource development—volunteers, board, and staff.
- Focus on all donors, not just big donors.

- Estate gifts come from donors at all levels.
- You can raise money even if you don't have a stable of annual donors.
- Asking for a gift that's too big is as bad as asking for one too small.
- We have no right to prejudge a donor's willingness or ability to give.
- Not all campaigns require a feasibility study.
- All volunteers need fundraising training specific to their organization.
- All gifts deserve heartfelt gratitude.
- Those who support organizations with similar missions are likely to support yours.
- Fundraising entails more than money.
- You may need a consultant even if you have fundraising staff.
- Even in today's fast-paced world, most donors still want to be cultivated.
- If your organization is struggling in its campaign, reexamine your case and your methods.
- Don't expect a windfall gift, but be ready in case it comes.
- The more you do it, the more rewarding fundraising is.
- There's plenty of philanthropy to go around.
- We're public benefit corporations, not charities.

ABOUT THE AUTHOR

Kay Sprinkel Grace is a skilled professional and articulate trend spotter in the nonprofit sector and a seasoned volunteer. Based in San Francisco, she is widely sought as a speaker across the globe. Her recent focus is on the swiftly changing face and fabric of philanthropy.

Kay's consulting clients span the nonprofit sector: public media, arts, culture, education, health, social services and the environment. Author of seven books on fundraising and boards, and speaker at recent professional gatherings in Italy, Poland, Czech Republic, The Netherlands, Slovakia, Australia and Canada as well as the United States, she has gathered insights and exchanged ideas with a wide array of leaders.

Kay has received Stanford University's highest award for volunteer leadership service, The Gold Spike, and was recognized with the Pink Carnation Award from Gamma Phi Beta. In 2013 she received the Henry A. Rosso Award for Lifetime Achievement in Ethical

Fundraising from the Lilly Family School of Philanthropy at Indiana University.

Find out more about Kay at www.kaygrace.org, including a full listing of her clients and publications.

Copies of this and other books from the publisher are available at discount when purchased in quantity for boards of directors or staff. Call 508-359-0019 or visit www.emersonandchurch.com.

Emerson
& Church
PUBLISHERS

15 Brook Street – Medfield, MA 02052
Tel. 508-359-0019
www.emersonandchurch.com